BRISTOL
BAY

BRISTOL BAY
AND OTHER POEMS

poems by

Gary Lemons

RED HEN PRESS | *Los Angeles, CA*

Book layout by Sydney Nichols

Library of Congress Cataloging-in-Publication Data

Lemons, Gary.
 Bristol bay and other poems / by Gary Lemons. — 1st ed.
  p. cm.
 Includes bibliographical references.
 ISBN 978-1-59709-455-9
 I. Title.
 PS3612.E475E53 2009
 811'.6—dc22

                                    2009029393

The Annenberg Foundation, the James Irvine Foundation,
the Los Angeles County Arts Commission, and the National
Endowment for the Arts partially support Red Hen Press.

First Edition

Published by Red Hen Press
Los Angeles, CA
www.redhen.org

For Nöle and Lila

For
Ever

Contents

". . . Oh I have suffered
With those that I saw suffer! A brave vessel,
Who had no doubt some noble creatures in her,
Dashed all to pieces. Oh, the cry did knock
Against my very heart! Poor souls, they perished!
Had I been any god of power, I would
Have sunk the sea within the earth or soon
It should the good ship so have swallowed and
The frightened souls within her."

—Miranda, *The Tempest* 1.2.5–13

. . . to thee the strife was given
Between the suffering and the will,
Which torture where they cannot kill;
And the inexorable Heaven,
And the deaf tyranny of Fate,
The ruling principle of Hate,
Which for its pleasure doth create
The things it may annihilate,
Refused ye even the boon to die:
The wretched gift eternity
Was thine—and thou hast borne it well . . .

—Lord Byron, *Prometheus*

KINGDOM OF EXILES

A man stands on the corner
Of a busy street asking people around
Him for help. His hand is out.

A small dog curls on an old army
Coat at his feet. It's his coat. Each
Of the faded medals acquired in exchange
For the rest of his life. The man is, what,
Hardly visible. The dog adores him.

There is a force between the man,
The dog and me. The shadow on us all.
It's an understanding about separation.
About night and day. It's two straddling
One. If anyone looks they remember
The man and the dog or they remember
Me. No one remembers all of it. Only
The bird flying. Not the sky.

The money in your pocket is mine.
The joy or sorrow in my heart is yours.
The muscle, the meat, the sloping
Line of that hill, the cold fog rising
From the wreckage of love. Ours.

I want to put my heart in his hand.
Instead I collect shadows, bring them
Home and drink what's left of them.
When I die I'll be the thing in your mirror.

AVIARY OF NOTIONS

Wisdom sits down to dinner disguised
As a guest covered with small birds.
The birds are trying to fly but are stuck
In the fabric of the visitor's adornment.

No one is happy, not the birds,
Not the other guests, not the table set
With candles or the freshly carved animal
With a knife in it—no one
Is happy when wisdom barges in.

If this moment were frozen
We'd see the birds are actually part
Of the guest, are eruptions from what,
In him, awakens that wants out.

We'd see the legs of the table tremble.
We'd see the oil from the flesh
Ooze down the knife into a pool
Where bread is dipped.

Speaking for everything
That's been deported to a country
Where love is hunted not for it's
Meat but for its feathers,

I say—wisdom does not deliver
Itself to anyone that will
Break bread at its table—this
Is the human folly disguised
As an aviary of notions—

At any minute the birds might
Break free to live in the air,
To sing a song note by note, tree by tree,
About a forest where everything hides until,
Following the song,
We come with our axes to listen.

Bristol Bay

Prologue

So many years go by before a thing
We slept with every night, awakened
To every day, begins to find its form in us.

A life is nothing more than looking back
To find the assurances to move ahead.
Did I choose correctly, was I wrong?

Fragments in the end. All the poor
Human heart and brain can conjure
From the sharp bite of each moment.

Let me say to you—hold fast to your
Lovers, take measure of their eyes, their breath,
Look at the pulse racing blue in their wrist.

You will forget it in the end. The long
Walks with your dog, the buttery sun
Falling across stones on a steep
Face you prepare to climb—driftwood
The next wave takes away.

Going back to this place is like that.
What I remember I'll tell you. What
I forget you'll understand brings tears.
Nothing is worse than forgetting.

1 Arrival

Shucked oyster for a month to get
The cash to buy rain gear and tickets
From Seattle to Anchorage to Dillingham . . .

Little plane tips out of the fog.
Two others and me
On board for a three month contract
On the floating processor, All Alaskan.
The Blue Zoo. An old body shipper
From World War II with the freezer
Converted from corpses to crab.

Plane comes over scrub aspen,
Touches down in a narrow strip
Of beach at low tide, crunching shells,
Wings digging sand as it waddles
Across uneven stones. Pilot doesn't care we
Almost die. Neither do I.

He takes off, gets air, rolls into the fog
So thick I can hear the ocean
But can't see it until my feet are wet.

There are noisy birds out of sight
Making the sound of a cat with
A bitten tail. There's a moaning
From somewhere, maybe another kind of
Bird we don't have where I live.
Maybe my dead grandfather saying
Son, go home while you can.

Someone has the good sense to light
A rooter and I pull out a pint of Old Crow.
We settle into the sand in the protection
Of beach logs, shiver in our gear
And exchange stories and vices. It's
Oddly serene, a few gulls, the muted
Sea, the lost battles and victories.

One of these guys is a skid row, down
On his luck ex-NASCAR wheel changer, the other
A former fast food manager fired for theft.
I'm the poet and am more or less expected
To say stuff like this: I rap on a rock
To get their attention—

"It is out of our powdered bones, our
Trembling wasted flesh, our inarticulate
Cries as the weight falls away that
The sun rises and the new morning
Begins like a curse still audible in a room
Thousands of years after it's shouted."

One guy spits chew in his cuff, the other
Bogarts the bottle and the spliff. Someone
Is running a chain saw somewhere. I hear
It but can't say where it's coming from.
I'm new to the ocean, did all my work
So far on the ground or up in the air.
Don't know a boat when I hear it.

But the other guys do—"must be our ride,"
Says the thief inserting his tongue
In the neck of the bottle for the last drop.

This beaten up double welded aluminum
Skiff edges out of the sea. Two
Harley Davidson guys with big hair,
Tattoos and bigger arms jump out,
Wade through the sizzling rip,
Take a long look at the three of us.
Guy says to me, "you'll do—get in the boat.
You two guys wait for the plane.
You're going home."

I get in the boat. They get in the boat.
We disappear in the fog to the ones
That remain. I feel right at home
Except for the ocean which is dead flat
And grey under the churning prop.
I wish they'd turn the damn engine
Off but then I guess we'd row.

"Why'd you leave those guys," I ask.
"They was drinking," one said. "This is a dry
Ship." "I was drinking too and far as I
Know that ain't a dry beach."
The one say, "yeah but you look
Like the biggest asshole. It'll take that
To survive the Blue Zoo."

Thunk. We bump up against
A long blue wall that goes in all
Directions as far as I can see.
"How'd you find this," I ask.
"We never left," one says.

A rope ladder comes dangling down
Like something a penitent might expect
After a session with the flail.
Guy says—"Welcome to the end of the world."

2 The Freezer

It was beautiful and ugly and loud and quiet.
It was gentle and rough, smelled of fish
And the sea roses that bloom in the waves
Just after the storm abates.
I went from picking fish to slicing them.
Then moved higher by going lower.
Into the freezer. A place Dante
Would have loved in a mirror.

The elevator door opens and the cold
Pours up the shaft and turns to rain
That freezes and falls like foreign coins
To the floor way below.
I'm in polar gear from head to toe—eyes
And nose exposed.
First floor is where all the action is.
Zero degrees.

The ship is rigged to run twice around the world
On the fuel it carries. We stay at sea for months.
Sell fuel to the crabbers and smaller boats.
Take on product from them too. All gets
Stored down below in one of the three freezer floors.
And in the course of our sailing it shifts
Or gets off loaded. We move it back and forth
To keep the boat in balance so it won't founder
Or slip too far over in rough seas. Then we drown.

Second floor same thing only the fish
Sold at various ports on the way home are here.
Not much movement. We're not going home.

The crates and boxes are silent. The pallets humble.
Second floor. 20 below.
The air is frozen and breathing is hard.
The voices at this level are just audible
Like footsteps approaching a house in the rain.
The dead fish elegantly express with frost-filled
Eyes their wish for us to join them.

Third floor. 40 below. Some king crab
From last season. Mostly empty. The elevator
Door opens and the heat brought from
The surface is swallowed the way the universe
Eats whole planets, whole suns and grows thinner.
Nothing is visible until the door closes
And the ice fog settles. No one comes
Here. I come here. Jesus wept. My tears
Freeze in my eyes. I see through their window
The twisted figures dancing and singing.
There is blood frozen to the color of sunset
On the floor and smeared on the walls.
Here is where the soldiers lay as the ship
Chugged home from Normandy, from the Bulge,
Loaded with an accumulate contribution
The world would never receive.

The infantrymen line up in rows and salute
As I inspect the wounds they proudly wear.
All are mustered. All are loved.

Today when I walk among the living I
Carry their frozen voices in my ear the way children
Carry pails of beach sand to a formidable
Structure the sea will erase.

3 Welding

I came here hoping to work as a welder
But there's already a welder so I
Do other things until the opening comes.
From picking to cutting to freezer hand
To freezer boss takes six days, pay raise each time,
And now, one week after climbing aboard,
I've got a stick in my hand and call
The Harley guys by name. No longer a slimer.

The boat is 460 feet long and made of steel.
Lots of work. 16 hours a day stringing
Cables through salt water and fish heads.
AC above deck. DC below. Shocked
Hourly, cold as hell and loving every fluid
Bead, every fire burning at the end of the rod,
Every volcano touched and lived to touch again.

One bad night I'm extending a catwalk
Around the Freon tank that drives the reefer
Unit. Wind is sideways, seas about thirty feet.
We're wallowing from trough to trough
And I'm having trouble keeping my mask on.
I lock onto the steel, strike the arc and begin
To push meltdown into itself to make
The strong welds that when chipped look
Just like bird tracks in new snow.

The catwalk breaks. The welder they fired
Was a boozer. He made the welds
I'm working on and they give way. Fifteen
Foot fall in pitch dark, the rod striking

Random arcs as it hits the side on the way down
By which I see the deck approaching.
When I hit I'm numb. Doesn't really hurt.
Someone hears me laughing, duck walks
Through the storm under the fallen iron,
Then goes to get help. Nobody around. Rain
Taking my blood to the scuppers.

I'm in the infirmary an hour later.
Medic gives me an ampule of morphine
For my back, which is purple.
Valium to sleep. Percodans for the pain
I'll wake up to. I sleep through the next day.
Eat the pills. Back to work in a brace.

I don't mind putting up with pain
As long as its tolerable and pays dividends.
I'm still the ship's welder and the lawsuit
I'll file two years later when I reach for an axe
And fall to the ground unable to move
Is just another small boat too far from land
To get home before water claims it.

But I'm careful now. Slower. Older.

4 Engine Room

Two weeks on the Blue Zoo.
Starting to learn the above ship.
Meals in the galley that never closes.
Big chunks of white cake with dyed frosting.
Lots of french fries, eggs, pancakes,
The smell of grease and spam, the walls
Redolent with coffee, nicotine, bright
Sharp agony of fish.

Table of poker players I don't know.
Oilers, engineers, big wigs, start yelling
At each other about their hands. I'm
On a break from fire, still seeing it
Crawl on my retina, drinking bad joe
And scribbling a poem on napkins.
Two oilers jump up from the card game,
Pull out knives and go to work.
When it's over one is on the floor bleeding

From a hole in his stomach. The other's
Been subdued with a chair.

We're three days steam from Dutch Harbor.
A helicopter medvacs the two guys.
Chief comes up to me and taps my shoulder.
I take off my mask and glare at him,
Steel in my eyes— he says, congratulations
Mate—you're our new oiler—finish your
Shift and meet me in the engine room—23:00.

The Chief has one arm. He lost most of the other
To a winch someone signaled to lift while
His arm was still in the tote. Left his
Arm among the wriggling, headless fish.
He uses the stub in fights. Sticks it
Right in a guy's eye. It's hard as leather.
Looks boiled. Sharp where the bone ends.

He takes me on the rounds I'll make every hour.
Take 50 minutes, 10 to log it, then back around.
Short two oilers so I'll work 24 hour shifts
Until they fly one in from Seattle. Probably a week.
Double-time over 60 hours. Damn right.

By the third night I've got it down. Chief
Likes me for not being stupid he says.
Says most them oilers can't find
Their ass if it was packed with uranium
And they had a Geiger counter. Shows me how to
Blow down the boiler twice a shift.
This is the big one. Boiler builds up too much
Steam it can go off like a bomb.
Told me he's seen guys dancing in the steam.
Writhing like lobsters in a pot, cooked
Right through to the marrow. Be careful
Not to misread them dials son.

I'm alone. Separated from the rest of the crew.
Eat with the officers. Live in the belly.
Don't get off at the occasional port—got to
Keep the old Nordberg 6 clean. I sleep

Standing up. Eat sleeping. Live in the wrack
Of cylinders, explosion of gears, hiss of valves,
So loud I'm partially and permanently deafened.

I find a locked door. Open it with a key.
Inside are co2 bottles for refilling the steering
Mechanism that runs off compressed air.
Door locks from the inside as well. I lock it.
Lay down among the strapped in bottles.
Sleep for six hours while the ship rolls
And thunders through 20 footers. Sleep
Like a baby. Like a dead man. Wake up and everything
Is fine. Skipped six rounds. Alive again.

Oiler arrives. I'm not going back
To my stick. Promoted to third engineer.
Chief rubs his stub on my cheek
Shows me the new ropes. How to
Take commands from the helm.
How to feed air to the captain.
How to do my part to bring the big
Boat into port amid smaller boats,
Pots and nets. 18 hour shifts. 8 off.

One night I'm wandering the belly
Listening for the voices in the freezer.
I hear them issuing from weird
Cracks in the plating, over the sound
Of canisters shifting, the noisy
Percolation of dreams gone awry,
Rinsed with offal into the sea.

I stand by the engine, feel it move
The ship, feel it in my chest, become
A being made of metal, filled with oil,
Responding to the stroke of cylinders.
Steer into the next wave.

5 The Captain

He never sleeps. Stalks at all hours.
White chin whiskers, seamed
As jerky, thin as bone, adrift in the air
Like a ghost very pleased to be dead.
I see him everywhere, touching a weld,
Holding fish heads near the conveyer
In a slant of halogen broken by shadow.

Yet the ship never falters in its journey.
Who is in charge when the captain is gone?
Some residual double at the helm?
Is he mated to the waves and steel?
Every thought a command whispering
Down corridors to the moving parts?

I am in trouble with my stomach.
I want to die. The waves are at 45 feet. The ship
Is almost going down on every wave. I am
Blowing down the boiler, trying not to puke.
It's 110 degrees in the boiler room. The dials
Waver as I hold to consciousness by a thread.

The captain walks in. Pats me on the back
Speaks to me for the first time. Says,
"Gary, she's blowing sweet tonight, blowing
God himself right out of the sky where
The blasted seiners will surely pull him
From the sea and, arrrgh, we'll have another frozen
God in the hold. Some say he's already there.
You hear the singing don't ye?"
Then he's gone. He called me by my name.

I talk to the captain every time we dock
Or at least I listen every time he sends
Commands to the engine room on the
Big brass clock that tells me what to do—
What he wants—everything between
Full stop and full ahead. He sits somewhere
At the top of the ship, pulls the lever
And in my world the lever moves.

We enter Kodiak. We're at quarter ahead.
It's hard to start a 480-foot boat
That only goes 8 knots top end but it's also
Hard to stop it. Each engine command uses
Air from the compressor. Each command

Requires the engine be restarted by air
Driven through a tube into the cylinders.
Like starting a prop plane by spinning the prop.

Suddenly the man upstairs appears to go nuts.
One command after another, each contradicting
The one before it—eighth ahead, full stop, sixteenth ahead,
Full stop, quarter ahead, eighth reverse, full reverse,
Half ahead, full stop. Each time I fire the compressor.
Shoot air to the Nordberg. It responds.
I can't see up above but I imagine
The slimers along the rail wondering what the hell
Is going on as the boat convulses its way to dock.

Then the air runs out. I get the full stop signal.
Can't do it, Compressor hasn't had time
To build pressure. Never happened before.
Chief rubs his stub in his eye, says shit.

Better hold on steady boys cause
We's about to hit something.

Boat glides into Kodiak. Big mountain
Towers over the docks. Three hundred feet
Straight up. Some say a tidal wave crested
The mountain and wiped the town out couple
Hundred years ago. Hard to believe a wave that big.

Boat can't stop. I can't make it stop.
Captain and I are hooked together by
A futility neither of us wants to share.
The commands come faster now. Full reverse.
Full reverse. Full reverse. Chief grabs
A stanchion. Wraps himself around it.
When I see that I grab one strut
Of the engine mount. Hold on.

The dock is full of activity. Big ship,
All Alaskan. Blue Zoo. Coming in with
Two months load of frozen product.
Front end loaders running back
And forth over the wooden planks
Bringing totes. Pallet jacks bringing pallets.
Men and women scurrying to get in position,
Maybe 100 of them, as we glide toward
The pier. One probably says something
Like—hey—they ain't slowing down.

We ride into the pier at a sixteenth ahead.
Slice it in two pieces like a knife
Through butter. Machinery falls into the water.
People fall into the water. The pier

Collapses like dominos in all directions,
Chasing those in the middle toward safety
Where it meets the land. Some make it.
Some end up in the water. Some are crushed
By timbers reeking of fish, creosote and gulls.

We continue. Glide into another pier.
Destroy it. Then we hit the shore.
Solid rock. Bottom of the mountain.
We stop immediately. In the engine
Room I'm torgued from my strut.
Thrown across the floor into the chief
Who is still holding on with one hand.
I knock him loose. He breaks the speed of
My tumble. We end up against the
Door to the CO_2 chamber. Nothing broken.
Chief gets up. Offers me a hand.
I grab for it about the time we both realize
I'm reaching for his empty sleeve. Phantom
Limb retaining the habit of courtesy.

We laugh. Alive and no fires. Go upstairs.
Up the fiddler. Ladder leading through a narrow tube.
Up four stories to the helm with a steel opening
The size of an oven door at each floor.
In case of fire in the engine room the crew
Can get out up the fiddler when everything
Is burning, exploding, dark with diesel smoke.
Enemy torpedo sliding through three hulls,
Penetrating, sliding through bunk beds,
Galleys, flesh— into the heart of the ship.
Going off with a flash of white phosphor.

We open the door into the helm. The captain's
View. Glass windows one inch thick. Below,
Tiny beings hanging from broken spars,
Swimmers in green current, floaters face down,
Machines in pieces, cargo everywhere.
Distant sound of sirens. Medics.

Captain looks at the chief—says, "I run her
Out of air boys. Trying to miss the
Pots and other entanglements. Run her
Out of air just like the dead. Look down there.
See the ocean come up against the land. The land
Wins in the short term. Ocean in the long."

One tear caught in his beard, color of oil
That needs changing, refused to fall.

6 Eagle

I'm stir crazy down below. We leave Kodiak
With our hides and a huge fine. Would've
Been worse but the crab pots captain tried to miss
We're illegally placed so the harbormaster took a hit too.
Tangle those in a single prop boat, steering
Goes and who knows what more damage.

Whole crew but me go ashore for two days
Drinking, playing pool, walking in the Russian
Churches, maybe praying to the Russian
Gods who it's said loved to dress in Alaskan fur.

It's not punishment. I couldn't have stopped
The ship. It's just that I'm lowest on the totem.
And the engine room is a disaster after the impact.

We steam on. Toward Dutch Harbor. Islands
To the east, smoking volcanoes, deep water
Under us right up to shore. Two more weeks
Under steam to Dutch. I'm now completely
Squirrelly. There's a blue sky I can't see.
Green water and tides with cormorant
Fishing the current, luminous creatures in the wake.
So they say. I watch the dials, make small
Movements with wrenches. My feet throb
When I sleep as if my heart lived in them.

Chief say—you need to get off the boat.
Go with Duke in the skiff for fresh water.
This is the job everyone wants. A reward.
We anchor close to a likely island. Hammer the

Waves with the Evinrude wide open.
Go ashore. I lay my face in the coiled
Grass like soft wire, like pubic hair just
Where it tapers to skin on a woman's belly.
Breath the secrets held there, the frost,
The shadows of gulls as they circle,
The wave flung sand and foam, the deep
Confidence of land no human wants.

We explore. Find a nice stream coming down
To meet the tide. Fresh water. We dam it
With stones and drift logs. I stay behind
To idle my way back to sanity while Duke returns
To the boat. Takes the thousand foot hose and drags
It back to the stream. Guys onboard play it out as
He moves away. It floats on the still ocean
In the little bay, trailing behind the skiff
In a fluid, changing line. The way a border might look
If the sea were divided by whales.

He motors up the creek and we put the end
Of the hose into the deepest pool
And signal the boat to commence pumping.
The line begins to pulse as the water
Fills it. On board, the other end is
Placed into the big tanks where fresh water
For showers, laundry and cleaning
Slime is stored. Then the tanks
For drinking water are filled and bleached.

Takes 6 hours to top everything off.
We have the line tied down. Duke
Falls asleep with headphones on.

I wander the island in search of signs
Someone like me has come before.

We're done. We free the line and the boat
Winches it across the green water.
Duke kicks the outboard over. I don't
Want to leave. I want to stay here
Until I fossilize and some other vessel
Finds me among vertebrae and feathers.

As we're leaving I see movement in kelp
Beds just south of our landing. White flag
Slowly raised and lowered. Something surrendering.

Duke steers for it. Adult eagle. Head
Barely above water. Exhausted.
Trying to fly with one leg broken. One leg
Hooked deep in the stink of a 40-lb
King salmon dead a week. Eagle tried
To lift it. Salmon tried to dive. Stalemate.

It stares at us from unblinking yellow eyes.
Screams a warning. The small waves from our
Skiff rise above its beak making it cough
And flap itself above water for a while.
Then it settles back into the kelp. Eyes close.

Even this close to humans it can't help but sleep.
"What are you doing," I ask. "Are you nuts?"
"Shut up," says Duke. "This biker's in trouble."

He takes his leather jacket off. Starts
Talking to the eagle, making sounds that
For all the world sound like a Harley
Shifting up and down gears. Moves the
Jacket closer. His hands are exposed.
The eagle watches. Duke drapes the jacket
Over its neck, begins to wrap its wings.
The eagle takes the flesh of his hand
In its beak, bites down until blood runs
Down Duke's wrists. He keeps talking.
The eagle licks the blood. Stops biting.
Duke lifts it up from the kelp, its broken
Leg hanging. "Now," without changing
Voices, untangle its claws from the fish.

I take its claw in my hand. Feel
Immediate surge of sky under wings.
Freedom like I never imagined drills
My senses. I want to cry. I take the claws
Out one by one. They quiver as they
Release. The air is still. The water is quiet.
Even the gulls have stopped their strident
Anthym. The last claw comes free.
Eagle snatches my hand, gently. Squeezes.
There's a little blood but he doesn't mean it.
Doesn't understand how soft I am.

Duke lifts him into the skiff. Holds him
Close to keep his restless wings still.
Eagle nuzzles Duke's cheek. No shit.
Stares that won't back down for nothing
Stare at Duke who stares it back.
I take us home to the ship where a hoist

On deck lowers a tote for Duke and the eagle.
He hand feeds it hamburger on deck until
Fish and Wildlife sends a helicopter. Duke
Goes with them, comes back the next
Morning. They took its leg he says.
Its gonna be just fine. They'll release it
When it's healed. Plenty of injured things
Making a living in the wild world.

7 Season's End

We had it all on this trip. Salmon strike
For two weeks outside Naknek. General Westmoreland
In the freezer pinning bronze stars on fish.
Stabbings, theft, whiskey, docks in ruin,
Death and above it all a one-legged eagle
Flying further and further from land in search
Of its friend. Swam in the Japanese current.
Volleyball between crabbers tied together.
Clinometer readings of 10 degrees. Dreams
Of the big bucks shattered like brine frozen
Fish dropped from a broken hook. Watched
Japanese inspectors suck roe from living
Herring for breakfast. Blood on their beards.

Dropped anchor and picked it up. Blue
Crab in Nome, Tanners in Dutch,
Herring at the mouth of Bristol Bay.
Stirred up the bottom. Dead fish everywhere
So somewhere people can lick their plates.

Little guys from the streets of Seattle
Who juggle in the off-season. Winos
Who come alive on a dry ship and hump
Their load. College students doing
The Kerouac thing. Natives walking in their sleep.
Assholes like me.

We come into port singing—the dead soldiers
In the hold singing, the fish in shining
Brine singing, the slimers in their scales,
The captain, the billions of tons of product,

The chipped welds and scalding pipes,
Singing, all of us singing with our eyes
Stitched open and our mouths completely closed.

Voodoo Economics

Walking the back country one day I came
Upon a bear cub surrounded by wolves.

The cub was making slow circles as the wolves
Snapped its thick pelt from behind.

They were playing with it before the kill.
The small bear cried as instinct raised its claws.

I'm no hero. I know this about myself.
But some things are worth dying for.

I ran at the nearest wolf and fell on its back.
My weight drove it snarling to the ground.

I stood with its neck in my hands, broke
It. Threw the body at the others.

They did not remember the bear. It was
Me and the pack and the occasional cloud.

They charged. I bit and stomped. They
Bit and tore. I gouged and swore. They howled and struck.

When it was over, when I was inside the wolves,
We went back for the cub and it was delicious.

The Log

A man finds a weight.
Big log—root wad like an open fist—half buried
Among long yellow grass above the tide line.

Man understands this is his weight.
Picks up one end of it. Drags it.
Puts his shoulders into it. Makes his
Back into a bow from which his
Breath expels the arrow of pain.

It moves. Heavily. Slowly.
Resisting his efforts, digging into
The sand, leaving a trail through
The yellow grasses that slowly spring
Up to cover the work of the man.

He's sweating. Into his eyes. Anger
Besieges cell walls, plunders the soft
Citizens inside. It hurts being this man.

He pulls it to the beach. The grass
Is gone but the sand is wet. It's different
But no easier to carry the log.

He stumbles. Falls. The log waits.
He picks it up again. Drags it into
The shallows, watching the movement
Of small blue waves that chisel
The horizon like ships
Bearing the applause of distant hands.

He finds the right moment, pushes
The weight into the receding surge of wave.

The log is free. It floats further
Into deep water with the man holding on.

The man can't swim. Now he's scared.
His body grows heavy. His clothes pull him down.
He climbs on the log. Log takes his weight.
Carries him. Back to shore.

Waking Up

Snow covers a mountain. Or the face
Of someone asleep on a mountain.

Truth circles in the cold flakes,
A bird of prey, waiting
For the sleeper to wake up, waiting
To gorge on the first lie uttered.

Is this poem about what is visible
And what is hidden? Yes, but snow has fallen.
The tracks in front of you are your own.

SLEIGHT OF HAND

He couldn't refuse the sky. It wanted
His last breath. It mentioned the
Thankless work of repairing air. Requirements
Of snow. Even though it was his breath,
The sky wanted it. Demanded it.

For the man the bequest signaled the end
Of all negotiations with fate to postpone
Signing the documents of surrender.

For the sky it was just another small wind
Consumed by larger wind—the dead man
On the ground, his last exhalation now
Under the wings of birds, the puzzled
Silence at the moment the magician
Makes the audience disappear.

In Memory of Nadia Anjuman
1980—2005

"I am caged in this corner
full of melancholy and sorrow...
my wings are closed and I cannot fly . . .
I am an Afghan woman and I must wail."

Dark red flower grown in the night.
Watered by sorrow in the garden of loss.
There—on the balcony above the empty tables
In the hot afternoon—opening.

I roll up my sleeves, taste the cold rains
Coming in over the tops of the hemlock,
Pick up the maul and go back to the wood
I cut into rounds this summer. It's dry
Now. Time to become fire.

I love this work, the huge, simple
Satisfaction of opening the fresh wood
With a quick stroke, the shoulders into it,
The breath holding the heart like a glove.

I just heard on the radio that Nadia
Anjuman was killed by her husband.
Another log halved then quartered.

Village elders sanctioned it. There's
Sap on my hands. I'm feeling the rain
More than I should. Unwarmed
By the effort. Cold somewhere
Blood can't warm. One more poet
Killed for understanding more than
Anyone wants to know about the nature
Of axmen and forests.

I sit on the biggest round and drink tea.
The rain has cooled it enough not to burn.
Think of my father and his hard hands.
Getting between him and my younger brothers
When the belt came out—taking their blows.
Was he like a husband to me?

This is not sunrise. It is sunset.
Beginning of the end of time, when
All things disappear, even to themselves.

I set the cup down and pick up
The maul—the work goes
On—and both hands are needed.

The Enemy Within

For Michael Robinson

I came at it from the front. Head on
The way our fathers taught us. It
Was up against a cliff, everything
In its life pushing it toward me.

I left it no choice. It declared
War on my soul and on all the souls
Of my family and neighbors,
On the souls of my wallet and horses.

It declared war on my canoe.
On the street lamp outside my window.
On the ironwork thick with ivy
Above the cafe where I read the paper
On warm, even cold clear days.

I had no choice. I fought with it.
All things caught in this conflict
With no voice other than mine
Assembled prayers on the sideline.

At first they cheered. The sparrows
Picking crumbs from the stones below
My feet cheered for a quick solution.

The songs of my supporters rang
Against the buildings with a different
Sound than they did against the bark of trees.

I came at it to the ovation of things
Caring nothing for the two of us.

But it did not go down. It fought.

I fought. We stuck in one another.
A fist like an arrow cannot be pulled back.
It must be pushed through.

We stop long enough to breathe.
We see each other, its
Giant hands and tiny wrists, my long
Nails and terrified hair.

Somewhere horses are running.
Somewhere an aria is played perfectly
And the breeze takes it across town
Where an elderly couple gets up
From their memories and dance
As the sun goes down.

When any two rub together a fire
Burns them both, burns the forest, tempers the axe—
Smolders under the skin like a ghost
Roasted by other ghosts for food.

Weapons fall from tired hands.
The enemy is defeated. We prepare
Two animals, one to carry the fire, one
To bring the winter home.

.

House of the Heart

for Pablo Neruda

1

It's late—very late.
I'm in my chair, watching the night
Spill ink across an empty page, seeing the table
Darken, waiting for you . . .

There you are old friend. Sit down.
Here's tea, the high mountain vines
Steeped 3 minutes, as you like them.
Please, strike a match

By this momentary light we begin.
Like lovers with fingers
Dipped in the rose of one another,
To draw the earth between us.

Strange how the same shovel used
In the garden will dig my children's
Graves. We consider this as another
Match flares, burns the fingers, consider
The voices of the sea reciting Lorca
Among driftwood and kelp along
The shores of a country whose
Alchemists render soldiers into gold.

Consider the pink boom of guns
In the conch, the voices of poets gunned down
In the tides, the future told
In the slow way land gives in to water.

War is red chrysanthemums falling on snow,
Writes a beast repaired by poetry.

2

Horses fly from cold
Barns in early morning light, wing bearers,
The mythological rescuers
Of children left in wilderness to die.

They come from the woods in mended clothing,
Silent as pack wolves, using hand

Signals to change formation, crushing melons
As they move through the garden.

Pause at the apple tree.
Where the old tire still hangs from a rope.
Lay down their guns— and swing
As apples fall around them in red rain.

When the very young are sent to war,
The countryside trembles in their fingers.

In all things there is fear of dying.
Stones cry as they turn to sand
Deer, at the edge of the forest,
Blood rising in their eyes,
Fear the breath of every shadow.

I'm not surprised neighbors report
Spirits in my garden pecking corn
And drinking from the gutters.

3

I see the curtain. You see the window.
Between us nothing is unnoticed. I
Tell you there is still blood on the highway,
Blood on the dirt roads and on the implements
Of harvest. You tell me of children
Pushing one another higher on swings
In orchards, of the poorly constructed
Mercies of soldiers eating local gods
As if appetite is a form of reverence.

Is it worth telling the unborn about
Animals set on fire by explosions intended
For them, how the cattle hissed in the cold optics
On an empty eye?

Death stalks the poem of the world,
The unwritten poem of each living and
Dying lamb. Observe the metropolis of a child
Shrink to a single empty street filled with
Derelict syllables left unuttered by love.

4

It is practical to sharpen knives. Many
Things require cutting. But the point
Is only intended to pierce flesh,
To lead the long blade into the unprotected
Place between ribs where the soul
Sees it coming and screams like a monkey
Understanding its human part.

In the doors of their houses, on cold
Mornings, farmers lick the edges of hatchets and
Prepare for the invasion of governments that swallow
Babies to increase their tribe, that plant
War on fields where scarecrows weep.

You sip the cooling tea, flicker into view,
Say—"nothing matters but the truth of the words,
The slick coat of the words pouring into
The pages like spaniels into frozen lakes."

5

The door slams open. Thugs in flag pajamas
Enter the room shouting patriotic
Slogans about honoring leaders
Locked in moral knife fights underground.

We are afraid. We have suffered
Through the long night with nothing
But the flare of a single match for light.

We have shivered in the cold room
To the sound made when apples stop falling.

Now it is morning. The house is violated
By voices coming out of the dirt
The way history bellows from the masonry
Of a buried arch.

The dam in the melons breaks. Blood
Seeps from the chandeliers, from the package
Of stationary by the cabinet, trickles from
The toaster—the house glows
Like the center of a winter rose, edged by
Rot, beautiful in glorious decline.

6

It is true in some places poets spend
Their days among flowers, among baked bread,
Not hearing the cries of field hands
In the crust, that goodness drips
From the comb of lovers pressed to
Each other in sunlit grasses while streams
Filled with fables murmur in their eyes.

We admire those who find love in these
Times. In our deepest place we rejoice
For the children who are touched only
Where a child should be touched.

We long for relief that doesn't come.
I know you are with me. You know
Love is as dark as it is light, that
The caress of pages turning is
A way to press our lips together and sing.

But damn it, guns in the orchard.
Lorca is dead and is killed again
Each time truth is enshrined, each time
Attraction to the sun diminishes
Obedience to the moon, each time
Tanks return to the armory with parts
Of students in their treads.

7

The end of everything is not necessarily
A climax obtained by plagiarizing history.

I said once that the door of the house
Slammed open and soldiers stopped
Swinging in apple trees and entered us
Like morning light.

I believe I called them thugs. That is
Unkind. They are our children.

If I did not tell you this I apologize
For it is essential you know about the smell
Of broken melons so any importance this moment
Might own is retained by someone alive
When the poem is done. Yes.

The captain enters the room, puts
Both thumbs around my neck, searches
For the source of poetry that lives in bullet
Holes and pecks his eyes.

The sun grows brighter, as if two gods
Collide and for one moment express one god
Before falling on the earth as night.

Only when the poem is written can
We see by its fire what's been saved.

8

You remind me of a story when we
Were children, how our village came together
To pull a stump from the common field.

Never mind that it was once the tallest,
Most respected tree in our poor country.
Never mind generations of wrens
Sang in it, that lions slept in it. That
Idiots spoke beneath it to themselves.

Experts in stump removal were called
Hands that choked a thousand trees to death, never
In anger but to slow the growth of shadows.

Through the planting season
The dead stump forced plows around it.
In winter the stump was a dark corpse
Humped with snow in a field without footprints.

You smile—"Spring fell from the cold,
As it always does, and my sister followed the trail of a red
Fox so filled with hunger for salt it took
Her glove from a windowsill. She was the first
To see the green stems uncurling from the stump
Like a penis from a president's grave.

She knows more of life than you and me
Will ever know. She knows the dark
Wood wherein a woman rises from snow."

10

I recognize the captain's rank as he
Grips my throat because he also touches

My heart with his sad eyes. He places
His lips to my ear and whispers your words,

pero de cada niño muerto sale un fusil con ojos,
pero de cada crimen nacen balas
que os hallarán un día el sitio
del corazón.

In the same room where your books,
Currents of your blood inside them, drip on
The carpet and stain it red.

We lift warm hands, sipping tea . . .
Smile at the irony of it—
The dangerous boy with justice shining
Like aquarium fish in his eyes.

The poetry written in times of fear
Is the poetry of wind through stone
Buttresses carved by water long ago—

It is the poetry of sickles hung
In barns, not knowing if they will
Cut October grain or the umbilicus
Between our bellies and an insane god.

The days disappear every day.
The frozen voices of the hunters
Trickle back to wounded prey.

Along the boulevards people place
Their palms to their chest when your
Name is spoken. They join hands and walk
Into the lilies hung from points of swords.

In the house of the heart, in the soft pink
Shell where the sea swallows its longing one
Wave at a time, children burn the pages

We write to stay warm, as if our words
Serve no better purpose than to warm a child.

Ebb Tide

Quilcene Bay 1985

Down to the cold sea in winter.
Four a.m. Intermittent moon.

The beach glistens with slack
Invertebrates the tide stranded.
I start at the high water line,
Follow the water as the moon
Pulls it toward deep ocean.

I'm on my knees in Helly Hansons,
A bottle of peppermint schnapps
In the big pocket with the velcro flap.
Not yet warm from the work.

I drag my empty onion sack
Through the mud and rake a circle
At the edge of the receding water.

Rake deep and the clams pop up
Like dirty nuts in the lantern glow.
Rinse them and put them in the sack.
Less mud, less weight to carry . . .

I fill four sacks some nights.
Forty cents a pound, eighty
Pounds to a sack, maybe $150 before
Sunrise when the bars open and I drag
Myself into the Whistling Oyster, fall
Asleep in rain gear over whiskey shots.

Each night I come to the ocean to die.
Each night I come to be reborn. Beyond
The glow of the lantern rain and wind blow

The sand into the pilings of an old pier
And whittle it to the waterline.

An owl cries from the shadowed coast.
An orca answers, come inland to feed
In the warm shallows, afraid of nothing
But impervious shapes adrift on water.

I drink peppermint schnapps
From my cold fist, throw back my head

And sing. I'm inside out, blood running west
Across sand, a parable of bones, drift wood.

I pull my heart from the tide before it's swept to sea.
Walk inland as my shadow swims away.

ANCESTORS

The sky surprised me.
I watched the light turn from hard
Yellow to amber, then
Empty of birds and insects,
Of falling leaves and dust.

Out of this simple
Clarity a bomb fell.
It came to the eye
As a speck reflecting
Sunlight in metal.

Two feet from my face it stops.
It's thinking. I can hear
Its thoughts tick in the
Oblivion it carries like a parent
Carries a tired child—

Did it explode?
I don't know. Did it land
Inside me? I don't know. I only know
I have unexpected moments
When I realize the garden died
But what's left is still a garden.

FAMILY

The rain falls on the lake.
Each drop strikes the lake
Then bounces back
To the sky before
Settling into the gathering.

I try to do this but have
No grace. Not that there's
Not the equivalent in
My life of open
Water overhung with bending
Trees. Not that there aren't
Birds reflected, stars reflected,
Sunlight sparkling, on
My bowl of rain.

In the depth of the lake
There is something that isn't
Rain that accepts
The rain, that takes
It in and deepens.

In me that might be god,
Waiting like a sunken log
For the arrival of a prayer
To float it back into a tree.

But it isn't. There is only the quiet
Body of water where we swim together,
As long as one arm is able.

Aerial View

Go figure why they died defending the
Annihilation of families driven
Into the crops like damaged tractors.

Why raggedy boys in butternut
Went out barefoot under their father's flag,
Marched in blood to lift that flag

In the face of Union cannon, dying
In stacks so high stables were made
From the dead to protect the horses.

After Fort Sumter it wasn't about slavery.
It got less complicated. Defense of village,
Northern armies driving into southern pride.

Those who survived grew up to see airplanes
In the sky.   Sitting in old soldiers homes,
Watching the wings cast fleet shadows

On monuments, dappling briefly
Hedges of roses and boxwood, they must
Have seen the potential of the aerial view.

Maybe they rubbed their wounds, dreamed
Of the Confederate Air Force, soldiers in
Gondolas dropping smudge on Union camps.

It's never about race. It's always money.
For every rich plantation owner, for every bale of goods
On docks from Norfolk to Charleston, for every

Atrocity committed near levies, in cane fields
And among filthy, uncombed balls of cotton,
For every hi-jacked drop of African blood,

There were a thousand desperate families
Dying in squalor in the dark hollows and piney
Woods of an America still here today.

Few care about the poor of any color.
Our history is blurred with miracles,
Horrors, compassion and lies—enough

Conflicting virtues and vices to stun
A passing angel from the sky where
Governments will interrogate it—

Until it reveals the places God hides
In our children. Until only children remain.

BUTCHER'S THUMB

Holding a burning candle along with
Half a million people gathered
To protest the Vietnam War,
I first heard the old wobbly
Song, "Joe Hill," sung by Joan Baez.

Each note built on the next, the story
Unfolding in the air, moving beyond
The bare cherries into the darkness:

"The copper bosses killed you Joe,
They killed you Joe, says I—takes
More than guns to kill a man, says
Joe I didn't die"

What does this mean to me
Forty-two years later, sucking
Loudly on memories like a straw
In an empty glass?

What does it mean to the many
Who speak, or the more
Who are silent, or the few who fall from
Their lives like young birds
Learning to fly before the impact.

It means we who resist are tired.
We who fall down are slower to rise.
We who love less likely to cry.

It means the gates to hell
Never close, the gatekeeper never
Sleeps, it means it does not take

More than guns to kill a man—
Guns are sufficient.

Nothing can speak more eloquently than
The bodies fired into the stones of cities.
In the derelict hour they shiver
Out of the mortar to drift among us
Like smoke from a burning tree.

They do not condemn us. Not yet.
They wait with their thumb on the scales
For the moment we arrive.

SPELL

Walk the perimeter without resting.
Everything will swell to dwarf you.
The importance and relevance of a single
Ant crossing the stem of a dead leaf
Brings tears to your eyes. Bones
Stick from the earth, break under
Your feet, mix into mud that cakes
Between thoughts like animal dreams.

Feel all of this and put it in a cup.
Add rain. Puncture a small vein.
Add what drips out. Place all your hopes
In the cup. Say them out loud.
Add the names of the dead. Those
You loved. Those you didn't. Exclude
Nothing that died in your care. Say
Their names into the cup. Your voice
Grows grass on their graves.

Add the ant. Add the tears. Pull
From memory the big disappointment.
Place it in the cup. Last chance to walk
Away. If you add the next thing every day
That follows will tick with the possibilities
Of a bomb disassembled for storage.

You're still here? Reach into your
Mouth as far back as it takes to get
Hold of the name of anything
You will die to protect. Put
This in the cup. Touch the ground.
With either hand. You're now on your
Own and the wrong choice will invalidate

The spell so stop thinking. Touch the ground
With the hand that wants to do the job.
If it's the wrong hand you won't wake up.

Touch the sky with the same hand.
Lift it as high as you can. When the hand
Is fully extended see which finger reaches
Higher than the others. Use this finger
To stir the content of the cup.
Drink from the cup. Every drop.

Be like a lion. You are alive. Nothing
Can harm you. Go into the house.

There is a room filled with strangers.
Invite them into the forest. Watch them turn
Into trees. Climb any one of them.
Become the grain in the wood. The spell
Is working. Any moment the leaves
Will turn golden and drop. In the bare
Limbs the hidden part of a child will
Stand out against the sky.

If the spell works you climb
Down from the trees knowing the truth
About yourself. The trees
Turn back into people who release
Birds from their mouths as they speak.

The old world breaks from the weight
Of feathers falling to the ground.

Orphan

The children don't care
Who made the bombs, who shaped them,
Whose dollars launched them.

It's enough to know the same light
That softens edges of hard days may
Burn through party dresses into bones.

People without families run.
Parents gather their children in their arms
And build a shelter from love that holds
Everything in but keeps nothing out.

Tomorrow the headlines will speak of a
Terrible pilgrimage made by distant
People toward a shrine that demands nothing
Less than everything they have as penance
For being born in their house, not in yours.

You wake in the night. A child stands in darkness
By your bed. She says, "I am your child."
Don't go back to sleep, this is not a dream,
This is the moment your suffering ends.

Fearless

You start with one small creature
Rubbing against your leg or in your
Lap purring as your hand strokes it.
Soon there are more of them—they
Must be taken outside and fenced.

They multiply behind fences.
More of them each day, pushing
Against the perimeter, wanting
Out, blaming you, their keeper.

One day, as you watch, the many
Become one and the one becomes
So large it eats everything in the field.
Then it eats the field.

You have only one choice.
Build a weapon from love.
Forgive yourself before you die.

QUIETLY, FOREVER

For Nöle

Under a shade tree
Beside a river of blood
We touch without speaking.

The sky comes closer,
As if drawn to reflect
In a pool wind never finds.

The river begins high
In the bones of elders,
Flows onward into
The deltas of children . . .
Imagines no ending.

Whenever we are tired
Or lonely, lost or gone,
Remember, we are together
Always, quietly, forever.

CULTURE OF SIGNS

When I enter cities I leave my
Skin at the border. Walk naked
As Eve into what became of a garden.
Something old takes my hand.
I dream of losing a bone.

There is a quality to the light
Piling against buildings like waves against
A barricade, a quality found
Only in paintings where the artist hurt
Herself rather than adorn the truth.

I am a bus in the rain, hypnotized
By each drop and the culture of signs.
I carry passengers down streets wet
With goodness that is the residue
Of screams. From a burning building

Shadows stumble onto the pavement.
There is blood where they fall.
Inside the building glasses shatter,

Voices are singing, music is playing
And men are holding hands
With the same tenderness and determination
Medics exhibit lifting stretchers.
No one is immune to the possibility of joy.

SECOND COYOTE

for Joseph Beuys

In a glass room the cloaked figure
With a shepherd's crook walks slowly
Through the scattered bales of hay.
In one corner a desert coyote
Licks itself and sniffs the air.

On the other side of the glass
Art critics applaud the coyote's
Spontaneous, one might say,
Natural way of relieving itself.

The cloaked figure describes
The atrocities of Auschwitz, the
Barbarities of Custer, cluster
Bombs, blowguns and burning
Jelly in a whisper
To the attentive animal.

Coyote loves to hear its escapades
Retold by those who don't
Understand the world as it is—
The moon in winter, the shrinking
Of everything into a patch of early light
Within which a small cub bleeds.

The figure continues telling
A wild animal of the sadness
Of a people who invented war,

Who don't understand
It is necessary, even admirable, to
Chew a leg off to be free.

The spectators grow serious, consider
Their fragility, the great orations
Of the action artist who places their
Story in the air the way a falconer
Flies a young bird from the wrist.

They applaud the moment from behind
One-way glass, going away
In small buzzing groups, less fearful,
Grateful to have witnessed the absolution
Of their next crime by one of their own.

When they are gone, when the lights
Are turned off, the hooded figure
Sits down in the hay, takes off its mask,
And the two coyotes howl at their joke.

What the Day Brings

A woman bends at the well. She pulls
A bucket from deep in the earth. Looks up
As thin lions glide out of the dunes toward her.

The village is on the edge of the desert.
The water is a thousand feet down.
The well is a thousand years old.

Sand creeps into the houses.
The crops grow smaller, the livestock fewer.
The wind rattles the ribs of the sick in their beds.

The woman lets the bucket fall.
It takes ten long seconds to land—
The splash makes one lion growl.

Everything is frozen. The children playing
Nearby are too frightened to run. Neighbors
Stare out of windows, relieved to be inside.

The lions charge. First slowly,
Padding the dust, then quickly,
Hungry for her . . .

To one, this woman is mother. One
Small girl picks up her stick, runs to the woman,
Stand between her and the lions and sings.

The lions stop. Consider the child. Listen
To the ancient words piercing the air like
Arrows aimed at targets still unborn.

The child sings. The lions sit in the dust.
The neighbors stare out their windows.
When night comes only the well remains.

Lost Boy

Where I was born the wind
Played accordions in the fields of timothy
That grew beside the corral.
Silver leaves on cottonwood trees
Danced above the shallow creek.

Hurricanes barreled in from the
Atlantic like drunken uncles in blue
Suits, spilling food and roaring curses
At the sky—the air turned green
And smelled of watermelon rinds.

Saw the roof blow off the barn
And sail into the house like a spectral
Alien craft. Draft horses kicked apart their
Stalls and ran in desperate circles until
We wrapped wet burlap on their eyes.

The wind showed us nothing is so
Unlike a window it can't be broken.

I traveled the world. Fought in jungles.
Jumped from planes, left them
Burning in the sky. Stood in corridors
Of universities with books in hand,
Caffeine-wracked over some damn test
Whose passing or failing meant less
Than fancy clothing on the dead.

I rode green ponies until I tamed them.
Caught them with sugar-baited snares.
Nothing is better than lying in the dust
Looking up at the grass belly of a young

Horse who pretends not to take interest
In you after stomping your spine.

I tried in my way to grow old.
I entered box canyons dragging mesquite
Posts and wire toward fences
Broken by the hard fist of days.

Now I ask you, in a whisper, to forgive
Me for strapping dead cattle to poles and dragging them
Back to our reunion under a sun so hot
The meat was spoiled when it arrived.
Solitude can make you do crazy things.

A door opens between the fluttering
Wings of canyon wren and the heat off rocks
Into a cavern filled with whirring clocks.

Ghost settlers, in ragged array, walk
Out of the dreaming red bluffs toward the
Bones of them left shining in the sand.

They seek the heart birds took away. The heart
Deserts shape to water found by singing bees.

Mostly, I've learned to touch that part, even to
Repair that part, without, often, killing it.

YESTERDAY

for Tim

The last log truck rolled down from the blue hills
Empty as the driver's pocket, chokers rattling,
Bed shifting, booms folded down and chained.

The driver parked next to the tavern. Walked
Inside, looked around at the crowd, probably
Enjoyed, as I did, the way the wood stove took
The cold from his face. Set down next to me.

I didn't say anything though I knew the look.
Out of work, out of money, out of luck. I bought
A round and we toasted better days.

He said—"they're all gone, every damn one of them.
Even though I hauled my share of them
I never saw it coming. Not an old tree left on private
Land and damn few on public. Must be how
Indians felt when the last buffalo was skinned.
Nothing left but to crawl off and die."

"I don't think so. It's different. Indians
Didn't kill the buffalo. The white man did and they
Didn't do it for food but to take away the evidence of god.
You guys did this to yourself and I don't mean
To put a fine point on it but you were mostly
Kept from the secret that the trees
You couldn't see were no longer anywhere to see."

He sipped his beer and didn't take offense.
Said—"yeah—you're right. Looking back
At all those landings in the early light
It seems those trees weren't real—

Were dreams—dreams we had for ourselves
And for our families, hell, for our country.

And we cut them down.
Loaded them on trucks, hauled them
To mills or ports where they were
Sold down river to a guy with clean hand.

I wonder if you can undream them. Undream
Those houses back to the mills, back to the trucks,
Back to the saws until the forests jump

Into the air again—don't suppose you could do
A thing like that and make it true."

But then what are dreams for if not to
Fill the everyday body with the hope that
Something truly miraculous flourishes
Beyond our war against tomorrow.

GARDENER

I never tried to be brave.
Let that be for others, or,
Come spontaneously.

I become emboldened when ice
Forms in late autumn on the dead
Vines whose fruit I ate all summer.

I am brother among trees pierced
By the beaks of birds or the metal fingers
Of saws—their sweet blood drips
Slowly from my frozen wounds.

When everything is prepared
I run to the winter garden,
Enter through the stiff gate, begin
To dance among the remains of plenty.

Dance, yes, little steps in sparkling dirt
While angels torn from paintings
Flap above the frozen rows like birds
Afraid to land because the scarecrows
Might be real.   And I am telling you,
We are.

New Years Day 2005
for S

1

I walk the streets today as I have so
Often in the last thirty-three years.
It's an arbitrary number to look back to
A place to start counting but my number
Nonetheless—thirty three years, the years of
Jesus, that good, misappropriated
Man, the years it took Conrad to begin
To launch dark missals at the human heart.

These are the years a man looks back at when
Winter comes not just to the place he lives
But to his body, left like last season's
Tools, one storm too long without shelter.

Cold wind comes off the water. Ferries
Labor in grey chop through mill smoke bringing
Tourists, seagulls, perhaps a younger
Version of me to town to begin, one
Hopes, a more fluid way to turn to stone.

I remember this feeling, these shivers
That comes from insights and under dressing
When I was a young poet walking from
One bar to another with a warm buzz
In Iowa City in the cold morning,
Late for class or early for another.
The arctic express came across miles
Of open prairie, bringing the smell
Of wheat stubble down from Canada.

There was frost on my face, fresh taste of
Breakfast beer, new words on my tongue.

Into the warm bar, Donnelley's, where Dylan
Thomas was slapped off his stool for cursing
By the same withered Irish prude serving
Me now, Charlie, who at sixty still rides
Home with his Mother who won't let him drive.
He sneers, brings me a democrat, a short
Draft with too much foam, would like to slap me
Too but almost got fired the last time
So contents himself with wiping a stain.

I believe in Iowa City each
Cold heart, each cold rustling stalk of corn
Left unharvested in the snow covered fields
Is warmed by a molten core of poems
Written by the dangerously young...

Music burbling under ice in creeks
Where coyotes cut their paws scratching
Holes in the ice to drink from the pool
Freezing slowly over the one remaining fish . . .

I still believe in the power of poetry
To make a place where one wild thing survives.

2

So I find my place in a world where war
Is killing my friends, killing people I
Don't know, killing any hope the old I
May one day become have of looking back
At their life to work out the intricate

Deception of a man struck each day
By a small, personal rock from space.

Because it's almost noon and I
Haven't eaten, I pour tomato juice in
My beer—it's 1972
For the first time today and *Imagine*
Plays above the tinkle of glass, the loud
Sounds of pool, sung by a man still alive.

Too much introspection from a drinking
Poet is like mittens on a cowboy
So I unstick myself from friends, the warm
Evaporate echo of words, tell Charlie
He's a beautiful man I'd love to kiss,
Dodge the bar rag, open the door on way
Too much light and real anguish.

I head west, a true conestoga poet,
To the Vine where Justice is counting
Money from an all night game and buying
Drinks for Norman who is building complex
Structures from pretzels and writing the last
Poems for *In the Dead of Night* on soggy napkins.

The new year has come, to the brave and the
Stupid, the ones who sharpen blades and the
Ones who grind what's cut to bread, to the good
And the evil, but never to the dead.

3

So here it is, thirty-three years later, thinking
Of my friend Sam whose new year will be a ledge,
Not a slope, from which he will fall or rise.
Thinking the fish breathes under water
Because it doesn't know it can't.

I have seen you breathe, in lonely places,
The fellowship that sustains and oppresses poetry,
Seen you daily labor with love, with
Great precision and joy, to extract the
Ordinary, infinite, thunderous
Relevant beauty from centuries of words,
Pissing off, in the process, those whose fuse
Is too wet to be ignited by ideas.

The first birds of spring fly just beyond the
Falling snow, waiting to land when my country
Thaws, waiting to begin the excarnation
Of my tongue, leaving only the bones of
Joy and one vowel, all that is needed
To begin a song of gratitude.

In everything there is the poem,
Stepping out of its own death.

This new year I have no pledges to keep.
I am doing all I can to be who I am.
To you I hope to say, at least once in
The remaining light, that I love you old friend,
Old teacher laboring in the garden.

4

When all the winters are added together,
All the summers, springs and falls of the oldest
Man or woman, we see they total less
Than the hair on our arms—this life is not
A nest we may sit indefinitely
But a single drop of water falling
From a clear sky that may, upon landing,
Give rise to a previously unknown vine
That itself will live only long enough
To take one fully awakened look
Around, flower, and then gently, without
Regret, remit its qualities to the air
And return to the work below ground.

What it all comes down to is, and yes, you
Can take this as a threat, if it gets
Any colder I'm switching to whiskey
Poured one syllable at a time into
That moment when the shivering ends.

End Game

1

In the beginning the earth was alone.
It had no language. Did not speak. Nothing
Disturbed the blue work of its dreaming.

It dreamed blood. Not just water.
Not just a salt filled basin of rain. Something
Momentary. Unable to feel anything
But the desperate ripple of its own stone.

Blood demanded blood. Killed just
To see itself drip from the ceiling in the room
Where earth dreamed rivers.

Let there be an end to lights rising
From windows, the smoke of machines, the
Crash of stricken roses as they fall.
An end to the cadence of hearts, an end
To bird songs. Let there be
An end to mothering the already dead.

The dream is over. Earth is awake.

2
Snake

Snake comes down the mountain with a ghost
In its mouth. Ghost feels no pain pierced by fangs.
Tells snake nothing is left alive. Only snake.
Snake don't care. Snake eats what's left.

When nothing's left Snake likes himself for a meal.
Snake hunts what oozes out of emptiness.

Snake finds 'em and pops 'em in his mouth.
Eat a dream before it finds a dreamer.
This way snake rules in a world without light.

3
Snake Dreams

Snake dreams of water. Seeing
Babies strung with seaweed floating
Effortlessly toward the sun.
Snake is alone with a truth
Worn so thin it has no sides.
A dreaming snake makes no sound,
Leaves no trail, weighs less than air,
Can't be heard, seen or felt by earth.

Snake is the last living thing. Earth hunts
Snake. Snake dreams and disappears.

But only for a while.
It must awaken. Then the clock begins
Ticking toward the time earth will
Feel the faint slither of the last blood
Filled tube moving on it skin. Earth
Sensing, snake sensing.

Before then snake will eat himself.
Snake will become the distance
Between inescapable beginnings
And inevitable conclusions expressed
By the dying sun over quiet water.

Snake will surface in the pink light
Surrounded by pale children whose
Hands are filled with bones that once
Were inside of them.

4
Snake in the Grass

Sure snake like a good slither in wet grass
But only if the grass is wet with blood.
Ghosts don't bleed so snake don't like em.

There are billions of ghosts, dandelion puffs
Singing as they fly, screaming when they land.
Snake moves through snowstorms
Of souls knowing his hunger is punishment
For worshiping god one bite at a time.

With snake gone the earth would be alone.
Understanding solitude, snake lives.

5
Snake Eyes

Snake has no eyes. Don't need to see.
Ain't nothing to see in the entire world
But snake hisself and snake done seen hisself
In the face of things he ate alive, seen
Hisself in the pool of liquid that came out
Of them when snake squeeze em good.

Now snake be blind. Sharpen his other senses.
Knows when to freeze, knows the voice
Of every dead soul hanging in the air,
Know especially when earth feels him.
Knows it be time to dream his self away,

Snake drifts through possible doors
Of awakening, not seeing, just knowing
When it's safe to be reborn.

Why do snake pursue another snake to be?
Why not give it up, go be dead? Stop hungering.
Be a ghost like all the rest. Be easy.
Just hold still. Let earth come. Let earth
Rise. Feel the ground tremble. Feel his belly
Sawed open by stones and dirt slide in.
Feel earth inside and no longer be snake.

Haw. Haw. That funny. Snake can't die.
Snake must live so not another world begins.

Why the Phoebe Wept

When I set myself on fire
The neighbors come to watch me burn.

Smoke obscures the sky. Lyrics
Like meteors scorch the streets and lawns.

What images can escape do. Birds,
My lifetime companions, fly

Out of the flames, lift on burned wings
And circle, seeing it written from there . . .

Small mice in the basement pop.
The little dog inhales smoke and sleeps.

The furnishings are nothing. They sizzle
And I laugh when they do.

Friends are worried but consoled
By the heat coming out of their clothes . . .

In the red coals, one word,
Unconsidered. Alive.
I pick it up. Breathe on it
Until I start to burn.

Notes on the Poems

"Bristol Bay": This poem is not a fiction—everything described occurred. There was magic in the landscape that spilled over into the temporary inhabitants. The gulls spoke eloquently in tongues. The seals grinned as they stole your gear. And an injured eagle nuzzled his savior like a parakeet. Honest. There were moments on the Blue Zoo that felt apocalyptical, like a Werner Herzog film. Fishing Alaska in the early 1980s had the feel of a liquid frontier town, where the bad guys were often looking at you in the mirror.

"In Memory of Nadia Anjuman . . .": Ms. Anjuman was battered to death by her husband who was embarrassed that she, a woman, was recognized as a poet of importance in her country by other men. The Taliban forbade women to write poetry and a woman who chose to defy them could be hung for it. The world is so much poorer without her brave being. I remember her, honor her, each time I sit down to write. The quote is from her most well-known book of poetry, *Dark Red Flower.*

"Second Coyote": Joseph Beuys was one of the most well-known conceptual artists of his time. In his performance entitled "I Like America and America Likes Me" (1974), he spent three days in a room with a wild coyote. He was met at the airport by an ambulance, swathed in felt and delivered to the gallery room without ever setting his feet in the United States. Each day of the three days Beuys spent with the coyote, fifty editions of the Wall Street Journal were brought into the room. The coyote acknowledged them by urinating on them. The coyote went through extremes of behavior, from aggressive, cautious, indifferent, to companionable. Beuys stated his performance was an attempt to communicate an apology to the coyote for the debasement it suffered at the hands of white men. The coyote was returned to its native country when Beuys returned to his.

"House of the Heart": This is an homage to Pablo Neruda in general, and in particular to his great poem "Explico Algunas Cosas, 1937 (I Explain a Few Things)." There are events so huge, so painful, they tower above us and blot out the sun. Neruda experienced just such a moment with the loss of his dear friend, the Spanish poet Garcia Lorca, who was killed by nationalist partisans at the age of thirty-eight at the beginning of the Spanish Civil War. The translation is by A. S. Kline.

pero de cada niño muerto sale un fusil con ojos,
pero de cada crimen nacen balas
que os hallarán un día el sitio
del corazón.

"from every dead child rises a gun with eyes,
but from every crime are born bullets
that will find you one day in the house of the heart."

"New Year's Day 2005": Woke up in the middle of the night, after helping my friend Sam Hamill move his old Chandler and Price letterpress out of his office at Copper Canyon. Sam founded Copper Canyon some thirty-five years ago and nurtured it with love and rigorous devotion into the internationally recognized press it is today. The Iowa City references, the Vine and Donnelly's, are places where I learned to drink beer with my friends and became the parody of a young poet it took me a number of decades to escape. The references to Dubie and Justice are to two of my teachers at the Undergraduate Poetry Workshop—Norman Dubie and Donald Justice. I owe much to both of them as well as to Marvin Bell for their patience and friendship during those rough years.

94

Gratitude to the following teachers who have contributed so much to my life and these poems:

Erich Shiffmann	Norman Dubie
James Lemons	Grady Gray
Terry Segal	Martie Lemons
Richard Miller	Helen Whittall
Larry Whittall	Bill O'Daly
Roger Lemons	Sharon Doubiago
Kay Freyling	Janneke Zevenbergen
Danny Little Bear	Anne Jablonski
Laura Pace	Jenny Van West
Tim Green	Hanno Giulini
Madelyn Curll	Victor van Kooten
Angela Farmer	Dirk Nelson
Carie Garrett	Billy Lynn

Thanks to the families Giulini and Lemons for their financial and spiritual support for the book as well as the poet.

Big thanks to Bill O'Daly for assistance with the Neruda translation. Where I have strayed or erred it has been in spite of his sage advice and warm guidance

And my gratitude to the good people at Red Hen Press— Kate Gale, Mark Cull, Steph Opitz, and Sydney Nichols. Thank you for believing in these poems.

Biographical Note

Gary Lemons has published a previous book of poetry, *Fresh Horses*, a CD, *Arisen*, and has appeared in hundreds of literary magazines since he was first published in the *Paris Review* in 1967. His poetry is a distillate of his experiences as an iron worker, Alaska fisherman, tree planter, and other hand-driven labor pushed through the filter of formal studies at the University of Iowa Writer's Workshop. He spent six years living on the Assiniboine reservation in Wolf Point, Montana, where he studied the Nakotan language and experienced the poetry of the open range. He now teaches yoga with his life partner, Nöle Giulini, at their studio in Port Townsend, Washington.